MOVIE QUARTETS FOR ALL

**Playable on ANY FOUR INSTRUMENTS
or any number of instruments in ensemble**

Arranged by Michael Story

Copyright © 2009 ALFRED MUSIC PUBLISHING CO., INC.
All Rights Reserved including Public Performance
Printed in USA

ISBN-10: 0-7390-6329-4
ISBN-13: 978-0-7390-6329-3

HEDWIG'S THEME
(From "Harry Potter and the Sorcerer's Stone" - 2001)

E♭ ALTO SAXOPHONE/E♭ CLARINET

By **JOHN WILLIAMS**
Arranged by MICHAEL STORY

Mysteriously

*A♯ = B♭

© 2002 WARNER-BARHAM MUSIC, LLC (BMI)
All Rights Administered by SONGS OF UNIVERSAL, INC. (BMI)
This Arrangement © 2009 WARNER-BARHAM MUSIC, LLC (BMI)
All Rights Reserved including Public Performance

33540

OVER THE RAINBOW
(From "The Wizard of Oz" - 1939)

Music by HAROLD ARLEN
Lyrics by E.Y. HARBURG
Arranged by MICHAEL STORY

Moderately slow

© 1938 (Renewed) METRO-GOLDWYN-MAYER INC.
© 1939 (Renewed) EMI FEIST CATALOG INC.
All Rights Controlled by EMI FEIST CATALOG INC. (Publishing) and ALFRED MUSIC PUBLISHING CO., INC. (Print)
This Arrangement © 2009 EMI FEIST CATALOG INC.
All Rights Reserved including Public Performance

AND ALL THAT JAZZ
(From "Chicago" - 2002)

Lyrics by FRED EBB
Music by JOHN KANDER
Arranged by MICHAEL STORY

© 1975 (Renewed) KANDER & EBB INC. and UNICHAPPELL MUSIC INC.
All Rights Administered by UNICHAPPELL MUSIC INC.
This Arrangement © 2009 KANDER & EBB INC. and UNICHAPPELL MUSIC INC.
All Rights Reserved including Public Performance

THE MAGNIFICENT SEVEN
(From "The Magnificent Seven" - 1960)

By ELMER BERNSTEIN
Arranged by MICHAEL STORY

© 1960 UNITED ARTISTS MUSIC CO., INC.
Copyright Renewed by EMI U CATALOG INC.
All Rights Controlled by EMI U CATALOG INC. (Publishing) and ALFRED MUSIC PUBLISHING CO., INC. (Print)
This Arrangement © 2009 EMI U CATALOG INC.
All Rights Reserved including Public Performance

33540

THEME FROM "A SUMMER PLACE"
(From "A Summer Place" - 1959)

Words by MACK DISCANT
Music by MAX STEINER
Arranged by MICHAEL STORY

© 1960 (Renewed) WB MUSIC CORP.
This Arrangement © 2009 WB MUSIC CORP.
All Rights Reserved including Public Performance

D.C. al Coda

EYE OF THE TIGER
(From "Rocky III" - 1982)

Words and Music by
FRANKIE SULLIVAN III and JIM PETERIK
Arranged by MICHAEL STORY

© 1982 WB MUSIC CORP., EASY ACTION MUSIC, THREE WISE BOYS MUSIC, LLC and RUDE MUSIC, INC.
All Rights on behalf of itself and EASY ACTION MUSIC Administered by WB MUSIC CORP.
This Arrangement © 2009 WB MUSIC CORP., EASY ACTION MUSIC, THREE WISE BOYS MUSIC, LLC and RUDE MUSIC, INC.
All Rights Reserved including Public Performance

HAKUNA MATATA
(From Walt Disney's "The Lion King" - 1994)

Music by ELTON JOHN
Words by TIM RICE
Arranged by MICHAEL STORY

© 1994 WONDERLAND MUSIC COMPANY, INC.
This Arrangement © 2009 WONDERLAND MUSIC COMPANY, INC.
All Rights Reserved including Public Performance   Used by Permission

THERE YOU'LL BE
(From "Pearl Harbor" - 2001)

Words and Music by
DIANE WARREN
Arranged by MICHAEL STORY

© 2001 REALSONGS (ASCAP)
This Arrangement © 2009 REALSONGS (ASCAP)
All Rights Reserved including Public Performance

BLUES IN THE NIGHT
(From "Blues in the Night" - 1941)

Words by JOHNNY MERCER
Music by HAROLD ARLEN
Arranged by MICHAEL STORY

Moderate blues

© 1941 (Renewed) WB MUSIC CORP.
This Arrangement © 2009 WB MUSIC CORP.
All Rights Reserved including Public Performance

THE PINK PANTHER
(From "The Pink Panther" - 1963, 2006)

By HENRY MANCINI
Arranged by MICHAEL STORY

© 1963 (Renewed) NORTHRIDGE MUSIC CO. and EMI U CATALOG INC.
Worldwide Print Rights Administered by ALFRED MUSIC PUBLISHING CO., INC.
This Arrangement © 2009 NORTHRIDGE MUSIC CO. and EMI U CATALOG INC.
All Rights Reserved including Public Performance

33540

PARADE OF THE CHARIOTEERS
(From "Ben-Hur" - 1959)

By MIKLOS ROZSA
Arranged by MICHAEL STORY

© 1959 METRO-GOLDWYN-MAYER, INC.
Copyright Renewed by EMI ROBBINS CATALOG, INC.
All Rights Controlled by EMI ROBBINS CATALOG, INC. (Publishing) and ALFRED MUSIC PUBLISHING CO., INC. (Print)
This Arrangement © 2009 EMI ROBBINS CATALOG, INC.
All Rights Reserved including Public Performance

YOU'RE A MEAN ONE, MR. GRINCH
(From "How the Grinch Stole Christmas" - 1966, 2000)

Lyrics by DR. SEUSS
Music by ALBERT HAGUE
Arranged by MICHAEL STORY

© 1966 (Renewed) TED GEISEL PUBLISHING and ALBERT HAGUE
All Rights Controlled by EMI ROBBINS CATALOG INC. (Publishing) and ALFRED MUSIC PUBLISHING CO., INC. (Print)
This Arrangement © 2009 TED GEISEL PUBLISHING and ALBERT HAGUE
All Rights Reserved including Public Performance